SKYWRITING

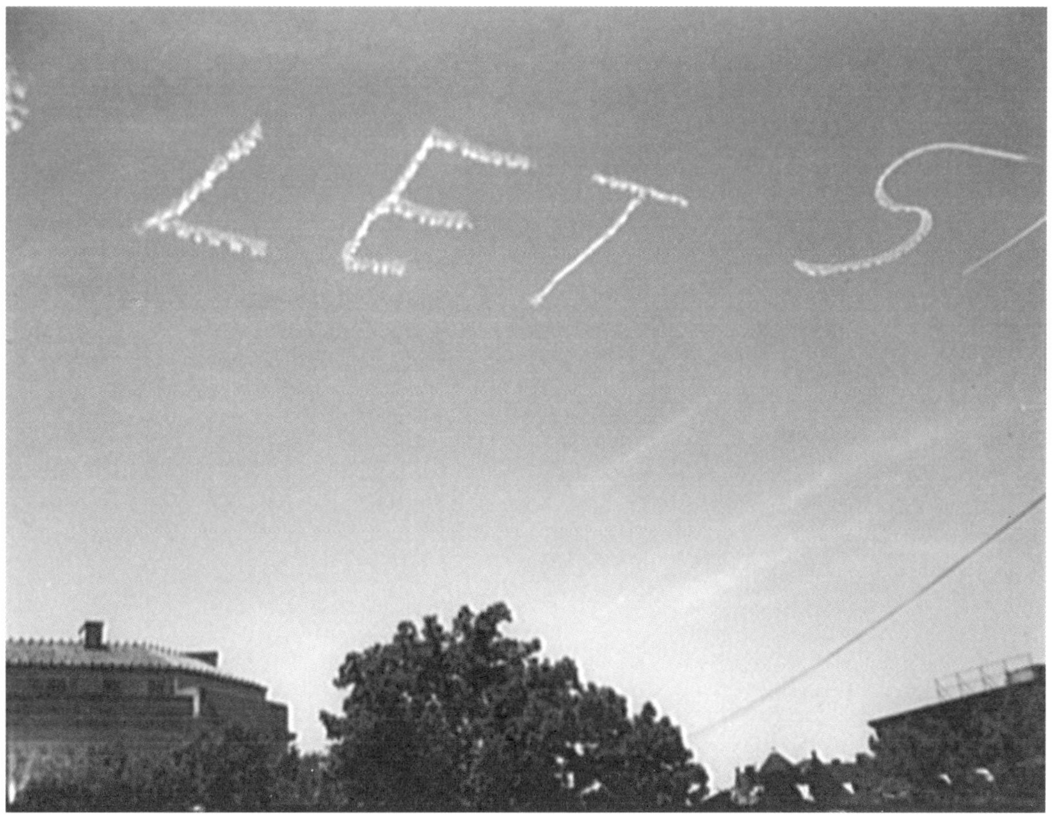

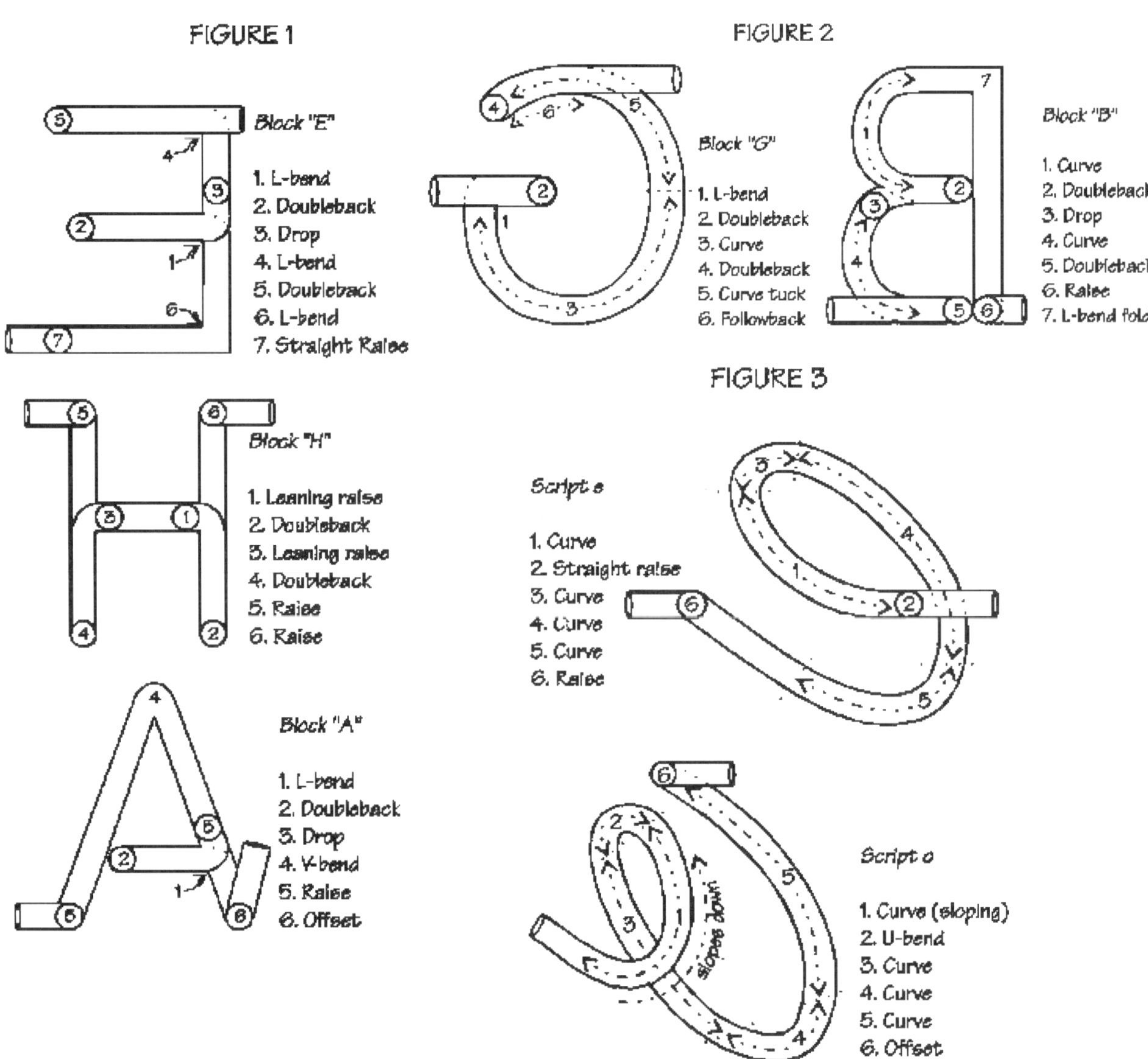
FIGURE 1
Block "E"
1. L-bend
2. Doubleback
3. Drop
4. L-bend
5. Doubleback
6. L-bend
7. Straight Raise
Block "H"
1. Leaning raise
2. Doubleback
3. Leaning raise
4. Doubleback
5. Raise
6. Raise
Block "A"
1. L-bend
2. Doubleback
3. Drop
4. V-bend
5. Raise
6. Offset
FIGURE 2
Block "G"
1. L-bend
2. Doubleback
3. Curve
4. Doubleback
5. Curve tuck
6. Followback
Block "B"
1. Curve
2. Doubleback
3. Drop
4. Curve
5. Doubleback
6. Raise
7. L-bend fold
FIGURE 3
Script e
1. Curve
2. Straight raise
3. Curve
4. Curve
5. Curve
6. Raise
Script o
1. Curve (sloping)
2. U-bend
3. Curve
4. Curve
5. Curve
6. Offset
slopes down

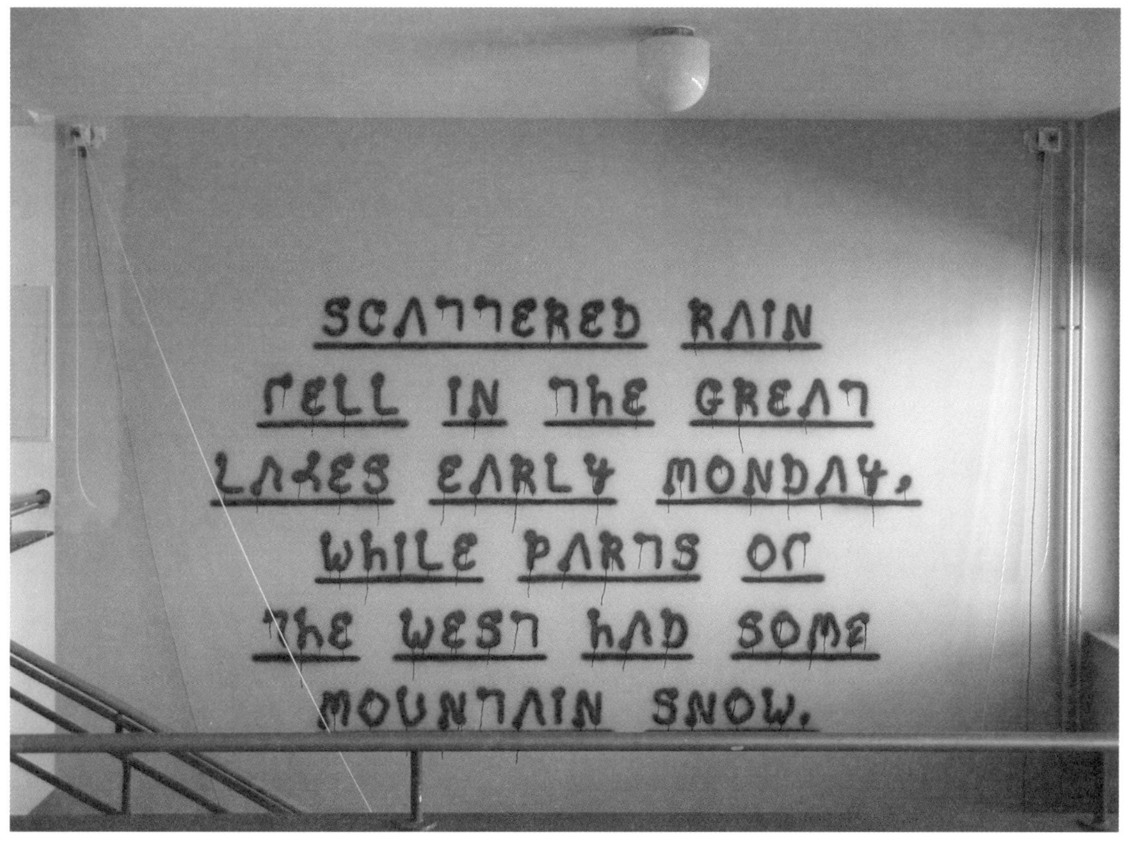

(Palm) Graffiti by Hektor

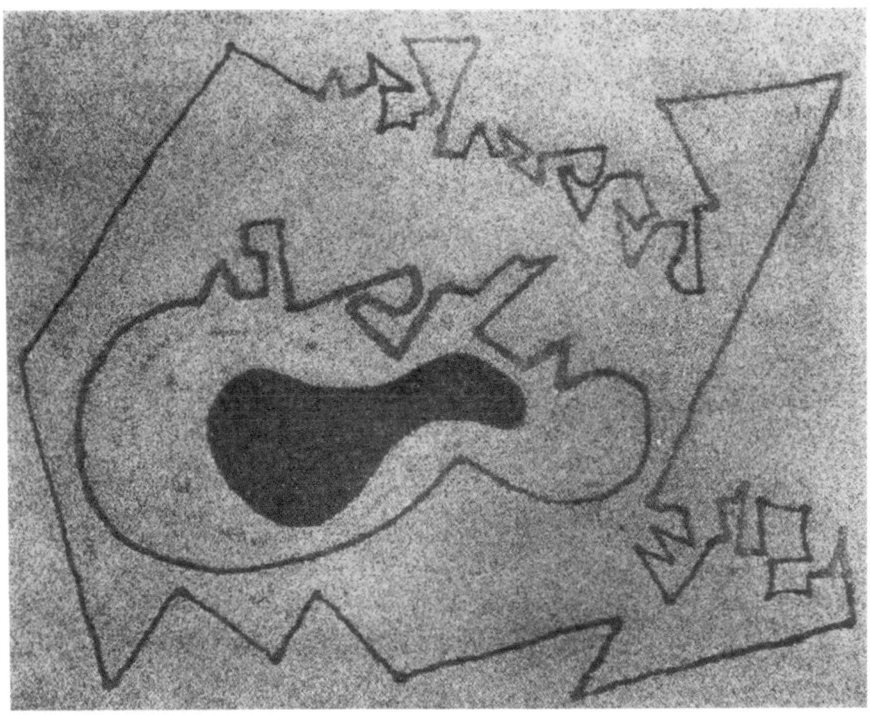

Fig. 11. « Ce Souvenir ».

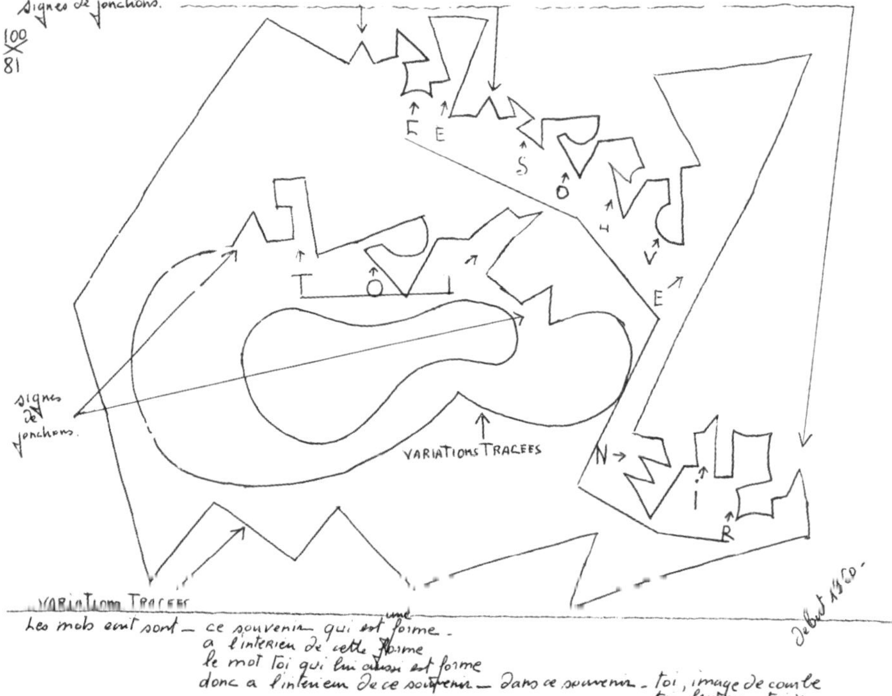

Sept. 12, 1961 K. R. ELDREDGE 3,000,000

AUTOMATIC READING SYSTEM

Filed May 6, 1955 4 Sheets-Sheet 1

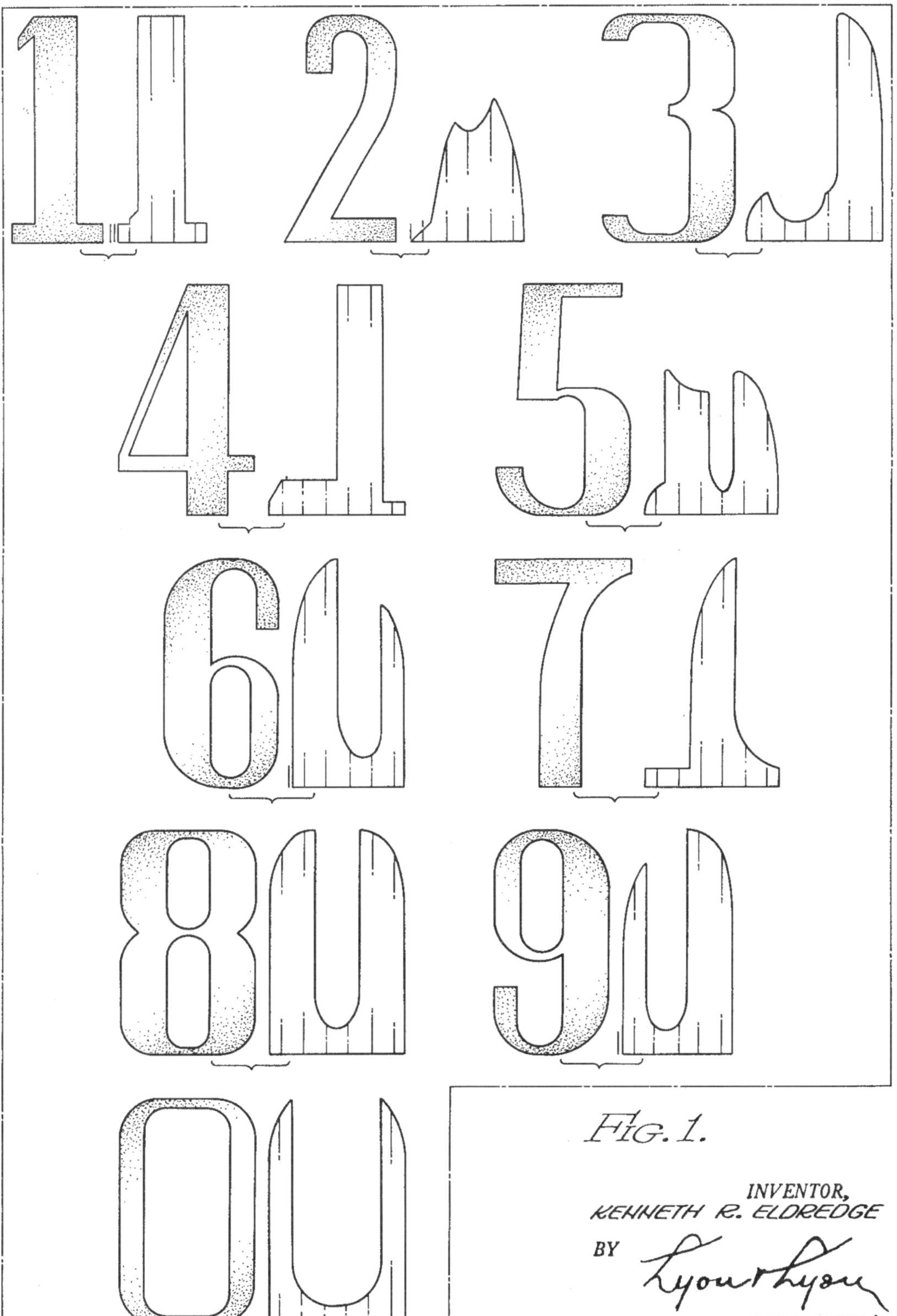

FIG. 1.

U.S. Patent Nov. 13, 1990 Sheet 1 of 51 4,970,659

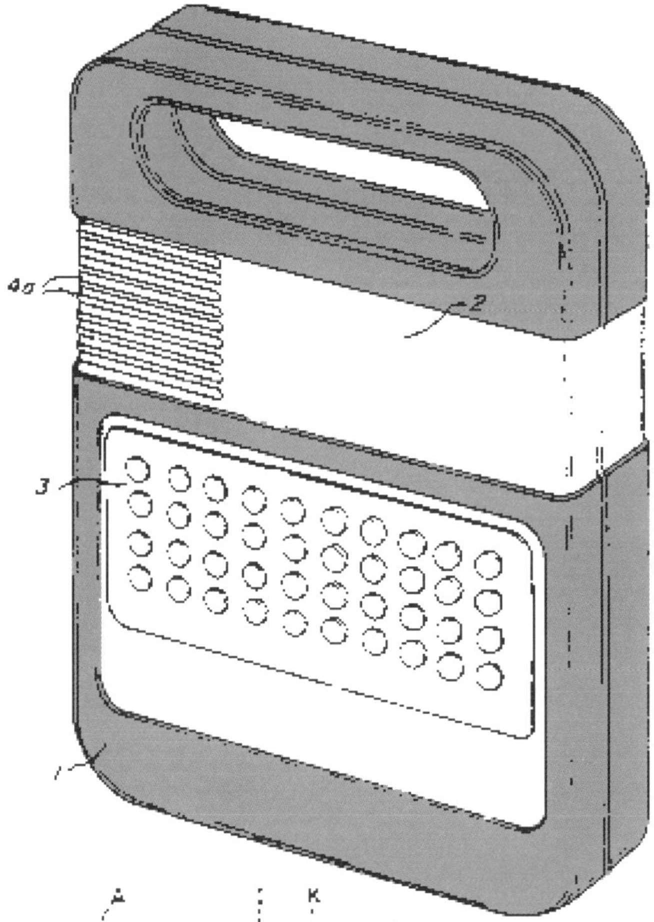

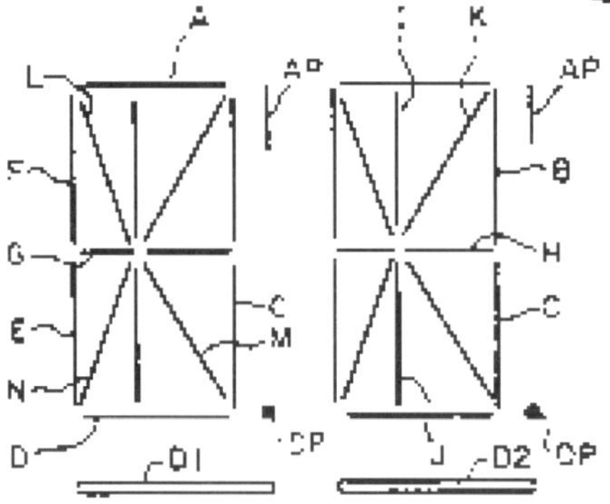

ORTHOPTIC STUDIES

louis émile javal

Louis Émile Javal, Physiologie de la lecture et de l'écriture, Paris, 1905

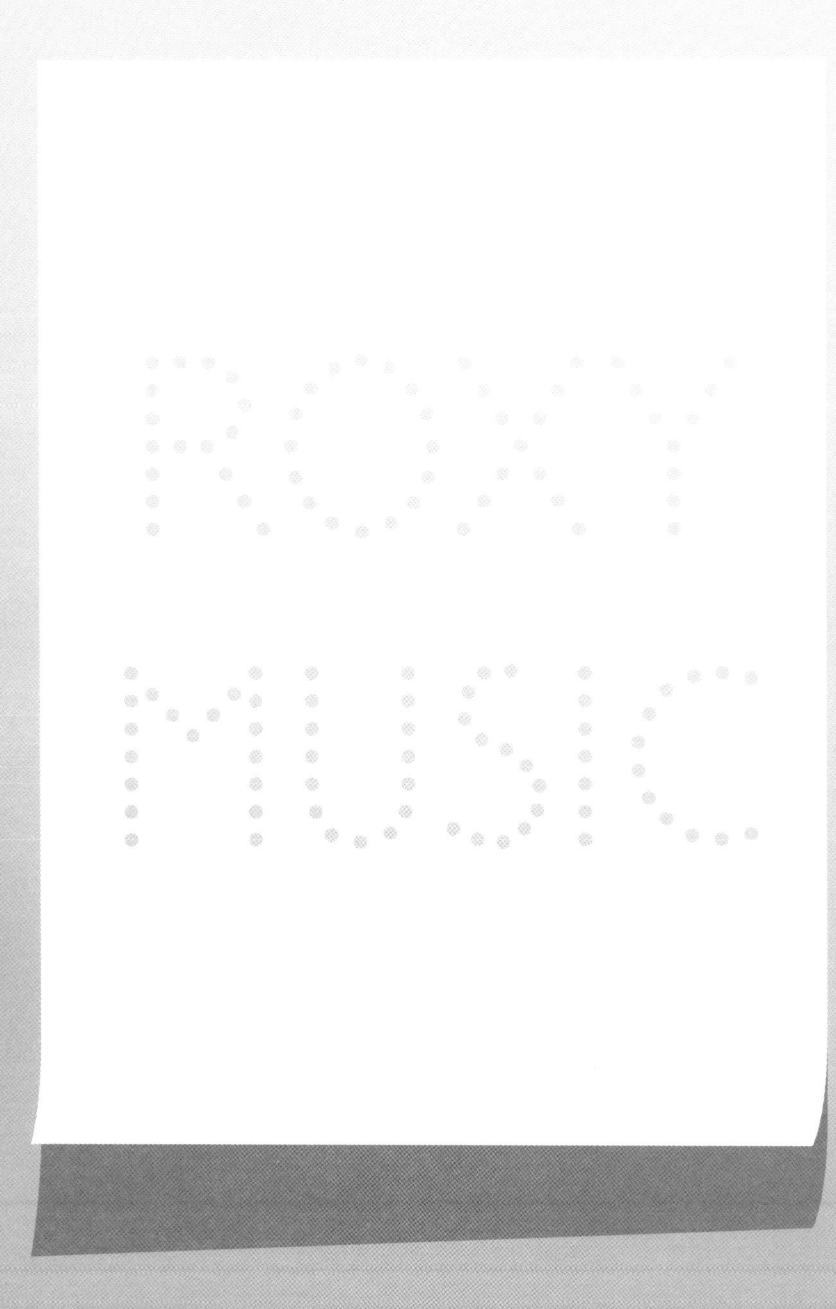
ROXY
MUSIC

Two posters for Richard Hamilton (after Marcel Duchamp) by Jonathan Hares & Alex Rich, 2006

MNEMONIC CHART

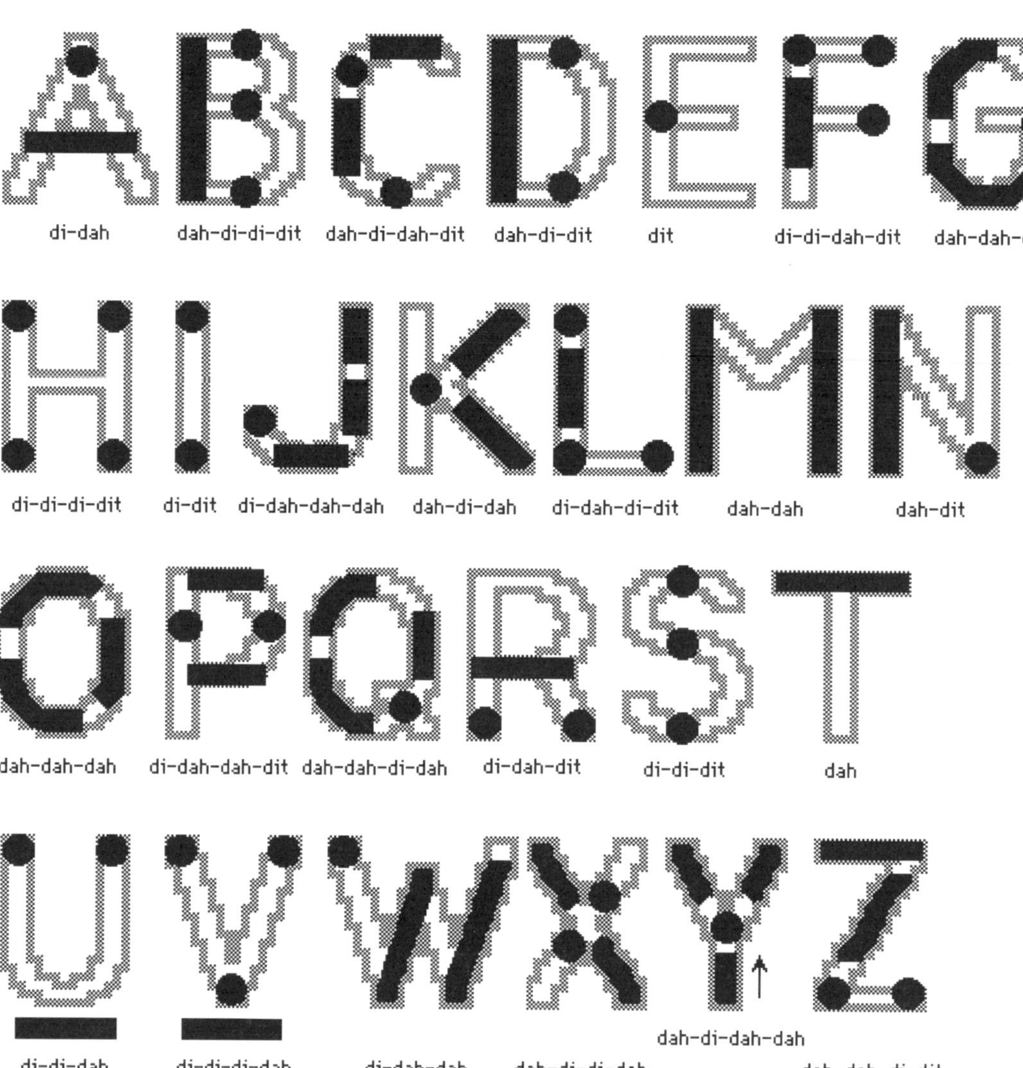

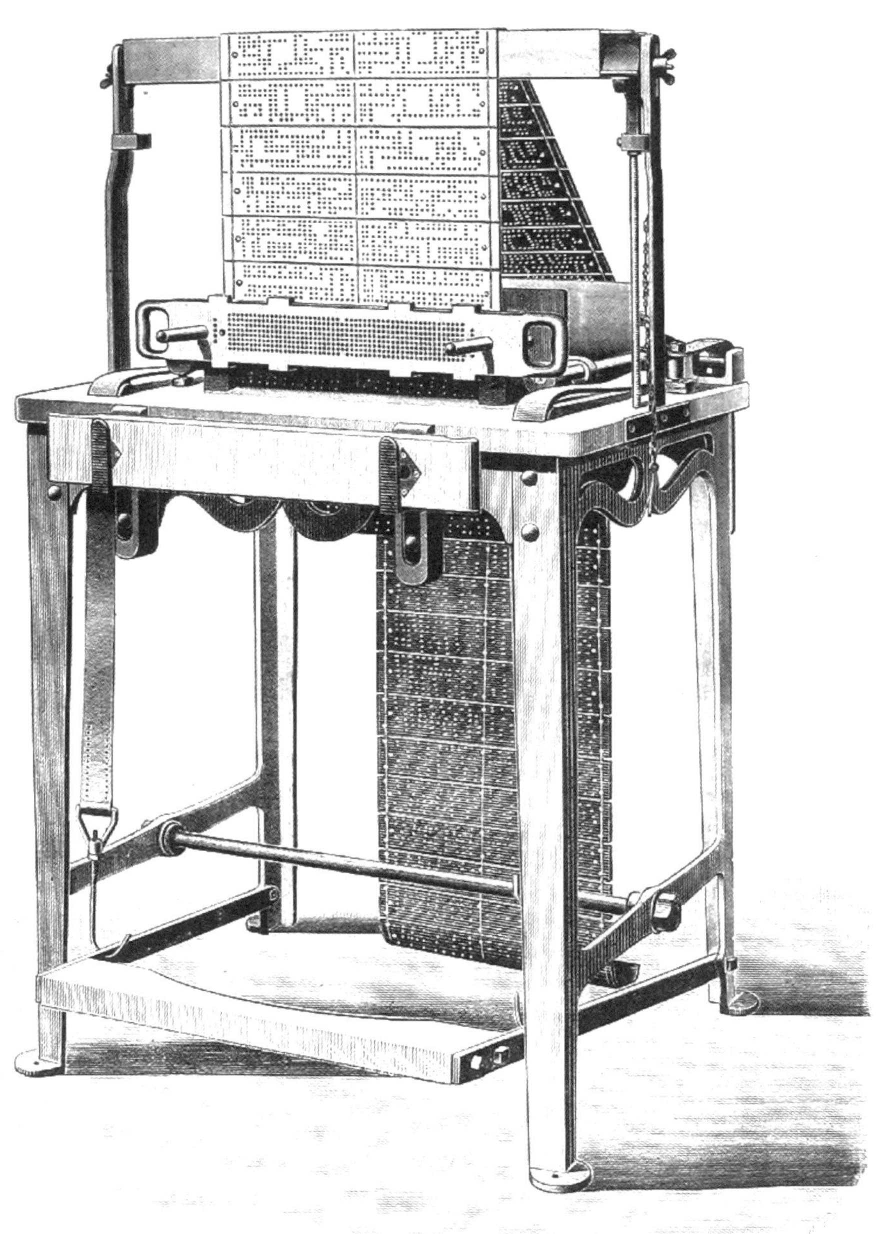

www.cs.uiowa.edu/~jones/cards/history.html

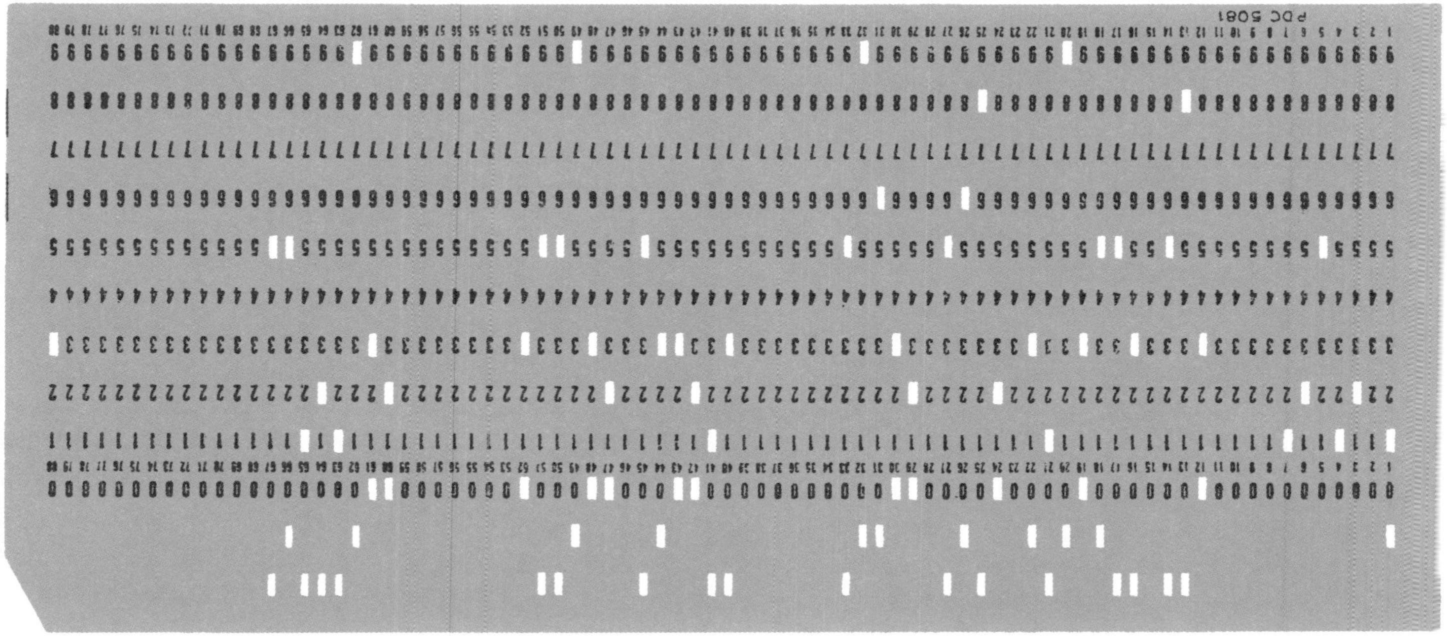

PDC 5081

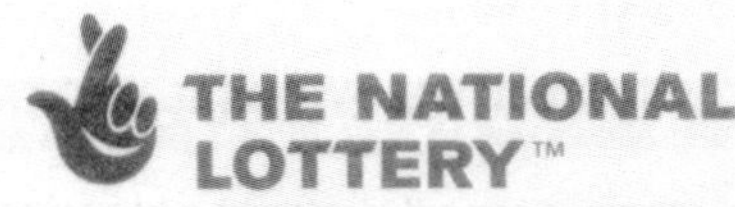

BOARD G £1 LUCKY DIP VOID

BOARD F £1 LUCKY DIP VOID

BOARD E £1 LUCKY DIP VOID

BOARD D £1 LUCKY DIP VOID

BOARD C £1 LUCKY DIP VOID

BOARD B £1 LUCKY DIP VOID

BOARD A £1 LUCKY DIP VOID

WHICH DRAW ? BOTH WED SAT

No. of WEEKS 2 3 4 5 6 7 8

IT COULD BE YOU!

SEE INSTRUCTIONS ON REVERSE SIDE

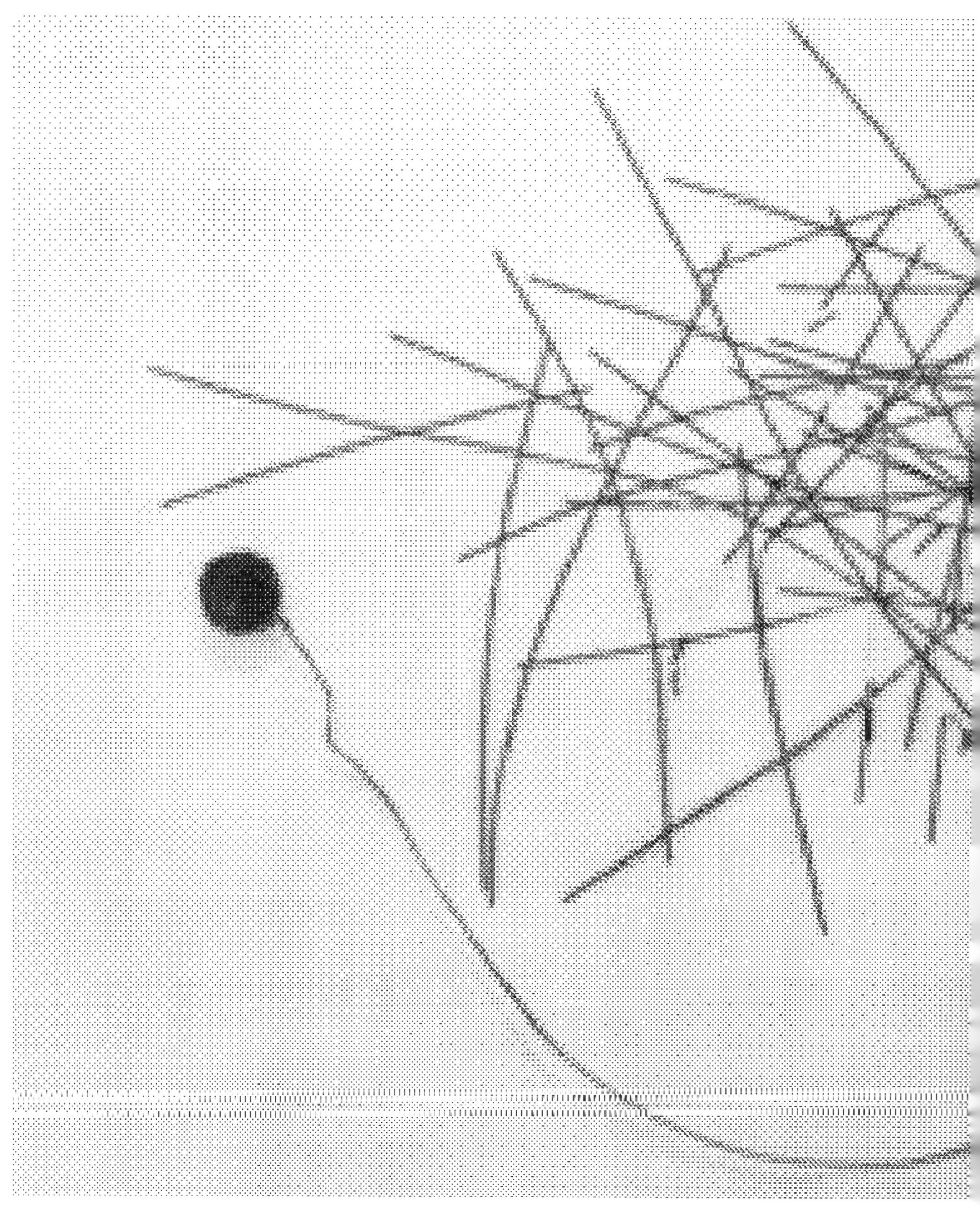

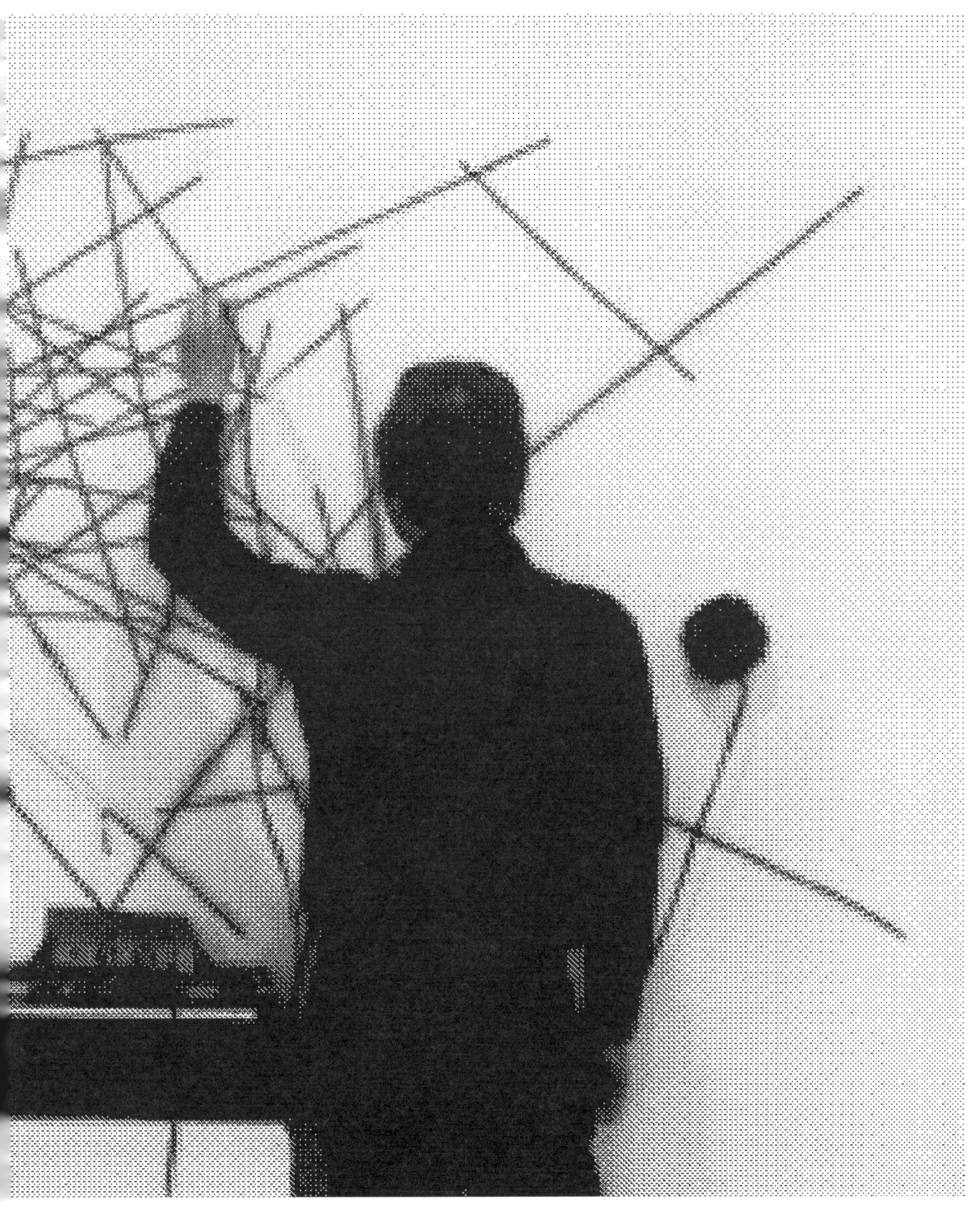

"ORDINARY" HYPERTEXT

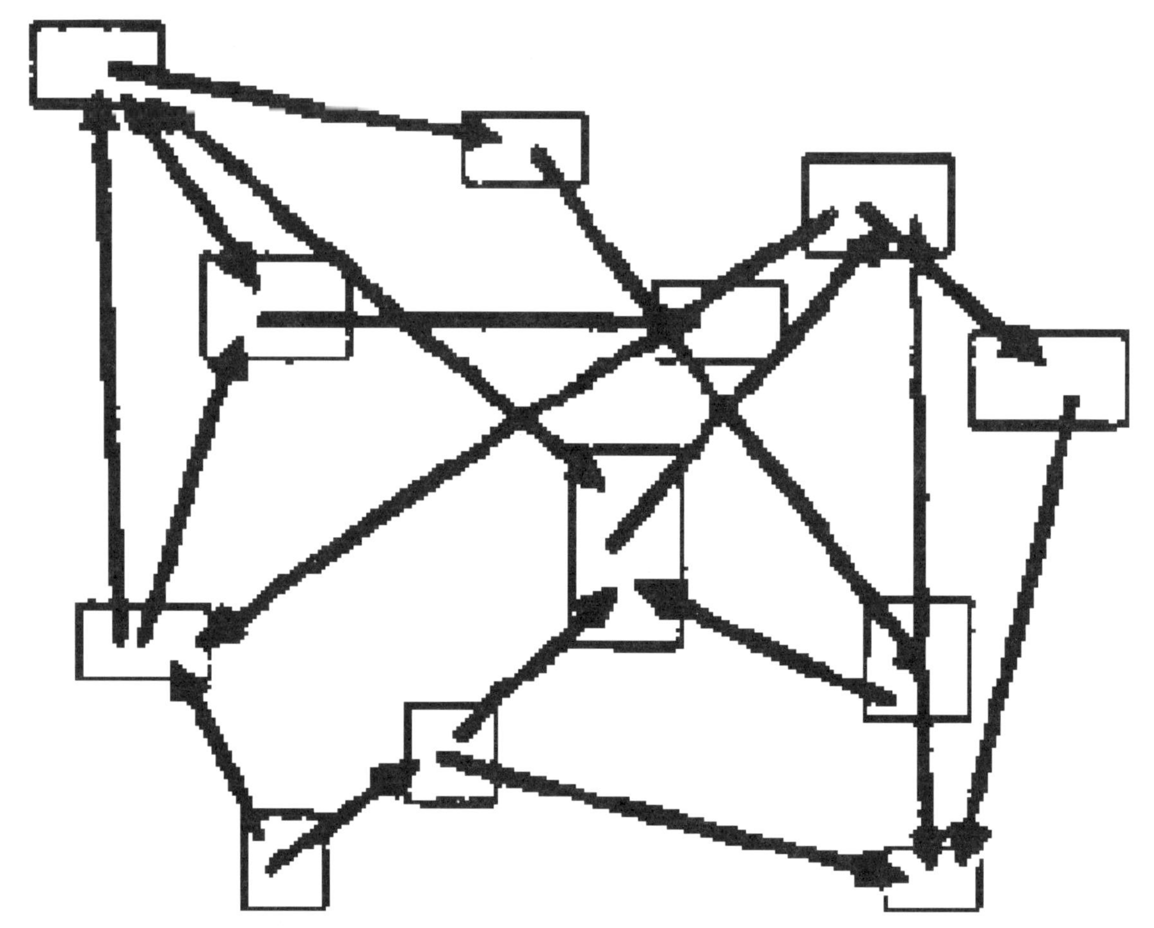